Fins
and
Legs

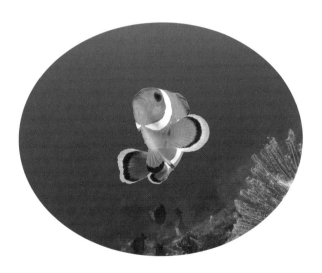

Written by Caroline Green

Collins

the dog puffs

a big leg

the dog puffs

a big leg

hens peck

· · · · · ·· ▬

a red back

hens peck

a red back

big fin

red rock

big fin

15

 Review: After reading

Use your assessment from hearing the children read to choose any GPCs, words or tricky words that need additional practice.

Read 1: Decoding

- Turn to page 2 and ask the children to sound out and blend the word **puffs**. Ask them if they can hear the /s/ sound the "s" makes. Then turn to page 6 and ask the children to do the same with the word **hens**. Can they hear that this time the "s" makes a /z/ sound?
- Turn to the "I spy sounds" pages (14–15), and say: Point to the **hens**. What else can you see that begins with the /h/ sound? (*hay, hat, honey, hoop, helicopter*)
- Ask the children to point to the **fork**. Say: What else can you see that begins with the /f/ sound? (*flowers, fields, fruit, figs, fish, fence, fox*)

Read 2: Vocabulary

- Look back through the book and discuss the pictures. Encourage children to talk about details that stand out for them. Use a dialogic talk model to expand on their ideas and recast them in full sentences as naturally as possible.
- Work together to expand vocabulary by naming objects in the pictures that children do not know.

Read 3: Comprehension

- On page 3, ask: What is the dog's leg like? (*big*)
- On pages 10 and 11, ask: What is near the red rock? (*a big fin*)
- How many animals can the children think of that have four legs, like the dog? Can they think of other animals that have two legs, like the hens?
- Ask: What animals can they name that have fins?